The 25 Universal Laws

That create love, peace, joy and abundance

Nicole Bayliss

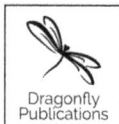

Dragonfly
Publications

THE 25 UNIVERSAL LAWS

First published in 2021 by Dragonfly Publications.

ISBN: 978-0-9875138-9-2

Printed by Lightning Source.
Cover Design and Layout: Ben Crompton Design

For information on ordering further copies of the book or to contact the author please visit nicolebayliss.com.au

This book is dedicated to all those
who seek a better life and a better world.

Contents

Introduction

This book is a small and simple book, yet it contains information that is powerful; so powerful that it can change every aspect of your life and how you perceive the world. These are the Universal Laws and they align you to love, inner peace and joy. These are the qualities that we require to live a fulfilling and abundant life. When we understand these laws and embody them, we have the power to manifest abundance, to love more deeply and be loved, to be well and to find and live our purpose. These laws will enhance our success and how we feel about ourselves.

So what exactly are the Universal Laws? Essentially, they are a set of rules which create the necessary framework through which to live life. These laws are set in stone. They cannot be negotiated, bargained with or changed. If we are working against these laws, we are working against love and against the Universe, but when we know about these laws, understand them and work with them, we have the Universe on our side and we step into our true power.

I suspect that some of these laws you may know already, such as the Universal Law of Attraction. Many people wonder why the Law of Attraction isn't working for them - the reason is that we need to know and understand the other

Universal Laws and embody them too. Each law is different, although some may overlap in their meaning and purpose. They are all just as important as each other. In this book I have attempted to present these laws in a way that flows, each lesson building one upon the other.

The more you can embody these laws, the more powerful you will become as a manifester.

Knowledge of Universal Laws has been talked about and written about since ancient times. You will read about them in the Bible, the Quran, and many other spiritual texts. While they may not be referred to as laws, they are described through storytelling. The Freemasons have held this knowledge for many centuries.

In the following pages, I will explain to you each of these laws and provide an affirmation to help you embrace the law. After reading about each law, I encourage you to contemplate how you can actuate this law in your own life

Wishing you peace, love, prosperity and joy,

Nicole x

1. The Law of Attraction

The Law of Attraction is the most well-known of the Universal Laws. It became popular in the early 2000's when the book The Secret was published. Other books followed, and many people felt more excited and empowered than ever before.

This law deems that whatever you think about, dream about, talk about or write about, you draw to you. So imagining what you want and feeling like you already have it creates the perfect vibration to bring about its manifestation. You can utilise this law by creating a vision board.

You can also use this law by creating a statement about what you want to manifest. For example "I am a highly successful entrepreneur who is happy living my ideal life" is a statement you could say every day. This affirmation is taken in by the subconscious mind which will go about creating this new reality.

The Law of Attraction encourages us to trust in the Universe as to the "how". Our job is to visualise and to feel that we already have it.

Affirmation

What I think, feel and talk about I draw to me.

Take some time to contemplate the Law of Attraction, ask yourself how you could best embrace this law to improve your life.

2. The Law of Abundance

This law deems that you have within yourself everything to create an abundant life. We all have, no matter what our circumstances. We live in a Universe of infinite abundance, but most of the population of the world right now believes in a world of lack.

Abundance is our divine birthright, but we have not been brought up to believe this. This isn't our fault. Our energy field contains ancestral traumas that have created the belief in lack and limitation. People do not believe possible what they have not yet experienced.

The Law of Abundance encourages us to have faith that the power already exists within us to manifest all that will enhance our lives.

Affirmation

I have within myself everything required to make my earthly incarnation a paradise.

As you contemplate the Law of Abundance, ask yourself how you can embrace this law to improve your life.

3. The Law of Pure Potential

The Law of Pure Potential deems that you have infinite potential and are capable of growing, transforming and expanding into ever greater consciousness, awareness and ability.

The best way to access your pure potential is through meditation. By going within, you will realise that you are not just a body and a mind; you are a spirit and a soul. Your spirit and your soul are connected to the Highest Intelligence, and you have the power to access and harness this Higher Intelligence.

You have talents and abilities you may not even be aware of yet.

The Law of Pure Potential encourages us to know that we are so much more than we know ourselves to be.

Affirmation

I am pure potential.

Take some time to contemplate the Law of Pure Potential and ask yourself how best to integrate this law into your life.

4. The Law of Process

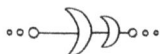

There is a process to manifest anything. There is a journey to getting anywhere that we want to go. Whether it is something that we desire or a solution to a problem, manifestation is rarely instant.

The ego wants to jump from "here" to "there". The ego is impatient and wants everything "now".

The Law of Process deems that certain things have to happen in a certain order so as to manifest anything. One thing leads to another, which leads to another, which leads to another.

The Law of Process encourages us to have patience with our goals and to enjoy the journey of life.

Affirmation

I accept that life is a process. I embrace the journey on my way to the destination.

As you contemplate the Law of Process, ask yourself how you could embrace this law to improve your life.

5. The Law of Divine Timing

This law deems that there is perfect timing built into every process. The Universe is in charge of the timing of everything; not us. If we consider how a rose blooms, it has its own natural timing built into it.

If we force it to bloom in a hothouse, it won't last long and it will have no scent. When we enforce our own timing on things, the result is not nearly as perfect as when we allow Universal Timing.

We live in an ego driven world of forced timelines and deadlines, which have created a lot of stress. Know that whatever you wish to manifest, there is already a divine timing built into the process and when you understand and embrace this, you can relax and allow things to grow organically.

The Law of Divine Timing encourages us to accept the perfection of the Universe's timing, and not egoic timing.

Affirmation

I surrender to the Universe's timing which is always perfect.

Reflect upon the Law of Divine Timing and how you can embrace this law to improve your life.

6. The Law of Surrender

This law deems that whatever we want - whether it is something we wish to manifest or a solution to a problem - we must surrender it to the Universe. The Universe is the Supreme Intelligence and knows exactly how to go about things. Universal Intelligence is well beyond ours, so when we surrender our hopes, our dreams and even our problems, the Universe will take charge and work it all out for us.

The ego views surrendering as giving up, and the ego doesn't like to give up control of anything.

Surrendering is not giving up and it's not throwing your hopes and dreams into an abyss either. It is "handing over" to the Highest Intelligence.

The Law of Surrender encourages us to let go and allow the Divine Intelligence to work for us.

Affirmation

I surrender my hopes, dreams and challenges to the Universe, knowing that it is the Supreme Intelligence.

Take some time to reflect on the Law of Surrender, and consider how you could utilise this law to improve your life.

7. The Law of Action

Intention is powerful, but so is action. The Law of Action requires us to take action that supports and moves us towards what we want, and not away from what we want. When we take aligned action, the Universe takes us seriously and we become a powerful co-creator.

The best kind of action is inspired action. Peaceful action or any action that feels good and propels us forward is also powerful. Stressful action or action that doesn't feel good isn't the kind of action that will serve you.

Take action one step at a time. The ego thinks in terms of giant steps, but there is no need to overwhelm yourself. Baby steps are fine. When the first action works out, choose the next and the next.

The Law of Action encourages us to take action that supports our goals and dreams.

Affirmation

When I take action towards what I want, the Universe takes me seriously.

Contemplate the Law of Action, and ask yourself what actions you can take now that move you towards what you want.

8. The Law of Least Resistance

The Law of Least Resistance requires us to take the path of least resistance whenever we can. We've been conditioned to believe that in order to get anywhere in life, we must strive and struggle. This conditioning comes from our ancestors, so it isn't our fault.

Taking the path of least resistance means taking action in a peaceful and joyful way, doing what we are able to do and when we come across a difficulty, we choose the path of least resistance to deal with it. Think of how water flows in a river - when it comes across rocks and branches, it flows around them. It doesn't go into battle and it doesn't know how to climb uphill! Water always finds a way, choosing the path of least resistance every time.

The Law of Least Resistance encourages us to flow and not fight; and to know that there is always a peaceful way to resolving anything.

Affirmation

I move forward with grace and with ease.

Take some time to contemplate the Law of Least Resistance and consider how you can use this law to enhance your life.

9. The Law of Challenges

The Law of Challenges deems that problems and challenges are built into everyone's lives because we are all here to transform and to grow, and we transform and grow through being challenged and resolving the challenge.

Through resolving the problem, we learn valuable lessons which we take with us into the future.

The Law of Challenges encourages us to embrace our difficulties, for through them, we transform and ascend into a higher version of ourselves and our understanding of life.

Affirmation

I accept that I will be sent challenges for my growth and evolution.

Reflect upon the Law of Challenges, and ask yourself how you can embrace this law to improve your life.

10. The Law of Acceptance

The Law of Acceptance deems that what we accept has the power to change, but what we resist, will persist. By accepting everything in our lives - the good, the bad and the ugly - we work with it and not against it.

Much of our unhappiness is caused simply by our resistance to having a problem or challenge. We resent it, we think "why me?", and we think "if only this problem wasn't in my life". When we accept life as it is, we are able to bring forth the solution. When we resist life as it is, the solution will evade us.

The Law of Acceptance encourages us to accept everything as if it were given to us by the Universe, because it has been.

Affirmation

I accept everything given to me; I resist nothing.

Take some time to contemplate the Law of Acceptance, and enquire of yourself where you are holding resistance, and refusing to embrace acceptance.

11. The Law of Perpetual Transmutation of Energy

This law deems that we have within us the power to change any circumstance. We have not been taught this; and most people in the world still believe that they are victims of circumstance. But within every one of us is the ability to transcend difficulties, and to transmute negative circumstances into positive ones.

The Law of Perpetual Transmutation of Energy encourages us to know that we are powerful and have the ability to change our reality.

Affirmation

I have all the power within me to change my circumstances.

Take some time to contemplate the Law of Perpetual Transmutation of Energy, and ask yourself how you could embrace this law to improve your life.

12. The Law of Forgiveness

The Law of Forgiveness deems that when we forgive anyone who has hurt or betrayed us, we free up energy that allows in our good.

We are all going to experience situations that require our forgiveness. Resentment, hatred, blame, judgement and feelings of revenge are toxic. They have a detrimental effect on the person who holds them, not the person they are directed at. These toxic emotions and intentions affect the heart and they prevent love from flowing within us, from us and to us.

We can walk away from difficult or negative people, however, if we do not forgive them, we will be presented with a similar person or situation until we learn to forgive.

Forgiveness doesn't mean that we condone what the other person did. It doesn't mean that we have to keep that person in our lives. It does mean however, that we consciously choose to let go of hatred, anger and vengeance so that we can feel light and free and move on with our lives.

When we forgive someone, we allow love to flow again which activates karma that was previously blocked. This is why people so often get their "come-uppance" after we forgive them.

The Law of Forgiveness encourages us to let go of anger, hatred and vengeance so that we can live our best lives.

Affirmation

Forgiveness frees me and allows me my good.

Reflect upon the Law of Forgiveness and ask yourself who you need to forgive and how you could begin this process.

13. The Law of Karma (or Cause and Effect)

For every action, there is a reaction. The old saying "you reap what you sow" is true.

The Law of Karma deems that if we do a a bad deed to someone else, that same thing will be done to us. It may not be by that person; it may be done by another person. Karma is not a punishment; it is the Universe lovingly giving us a necessary lesson.

We are told in the Bible "Do unto others as you would wish them to do unto you". The Universe keeps the score. We don't get away with anything!

Conversely, our good deeds are also taken into account and create positive karma. Much of what we see as "good luck" or "a stroke of fortune" is actually an accumulation of good karma from good deeds done in the past.

The Law of Karma encourages us to be mindful of our actions and our words, as the Universe keeps the score.

Affirmation

I reap what I sow.

Take some time to reflect upon the Law of Karma and ask yourself how you could use this law to enhance your life.

14. The Law of Replacement

The Law of Replacement deems that if you experience a loss of any kind, the loss will be replaced by something the same or better. Energy cannot die; it can only be transmuted into something else.

The ego believes in loss; it does not trust that everything will be replenished. If we choose to believe in loss, we block the energy of replacement from flowing to us. When we trust that the loss will be replaced, it shall come to us in divine and perfect timing.

The Law of Replacement encourages us to trust that all will be replaced in divine and perfect timing.

Affirmation

All is replaced and replenished in divine and perfect timing.

Reflect upon the Law of Replacement and ask yourself how you can use this law to enhance your life.

15. The Law of Divine Compensation

The Law of Divine Compensation deems that if we make a mistake and experience a loss or negative outcome from that mistake, we shall receive divine compensation from the Universe if we:

a. Own our part in it and learn the necessary lesson

b. Forgive all those involved including ourselves.

If we resent the situation and do not take responsibility for our part in it, we block Divine Compensation. Energy is never lost; it is only ever transmuted. Divine Compensation arrives when we have taken responsibility and forgiven ourselves and others.

The Law of Divine Compensation encourages us to trust that we will be divinely compensated when we learn our lesson and forgive ourselves and others.

Affirmation

All losses are replenished when I take responsibility and forgive.

Contemplate the Law of Divine Compensation and ask yourself how you can utilise this law to enhance your life.

16. The Law of Giving and Receiving

The Law of Giving and Receiving deems that the Universe works on exchange, and that whatever we are willing to give away will return to us, sometimes manifold. If we give money away to a good cause, we will get even more back, however if we put money towards something not in our highest good, it is unlikely to return to us. This is why drug addicts usually become broke.

We must learn to give and receive in equal measure. Some people are more comfortable receiving but not giving; others want to receive and not give. If you tend to attract "takers", then your work is to be more willing to receive and give a little less. And if you attract those who give too much, your work is to be more willing to give yourself and receive a little less.

If there is something you are really wanting to manifest, you've got to give whatever that is away first. And if there is something you really want to give away, you must learn to receive it first.

The Law of Giving and Receiving encourages us to both give and receive.

Affirmation

I lovingly give and I lovingly receive in equal measure.

Take some time to contemplate the Law of Giving and Receiving, and ask yourself how you can work with this law so as to improve your life.

17. The Law of Balance

Everything has its polarities - hot and cold, left and right, dark and light, rich and poor. When we become extreme in anything, we actually lose our power. When we choose the middle way, we are in full power. The Law of Balance deems that when we seek balance, we feel balanced.

Think of how a boat sails - it requires just the right tension in its sails so as to move against the wind. As human beings, we do well when we feel balanced, and seek balance in all areas of our lives such as:

- Work vs personal time
- Time alone vs social connection
- Freedom vs obligations
- Rest vs activity
- Spirituality vs earthly action.

The Law of Balance encourages us to seek balance in all things.

Affirmation

I aim for balance in all things.

Reflect upon the Law of Balance and enquire within yourself how you can embrace this law to improve your life.

18. The Law of Rhythm

The Law of Rhythm deems that there is "a time for all things under Heaven". Consider the seasons, which are cyclical. Look at how the tide moves in and out according to the cycles of the moon.

In the Bible we are told "To everything there is a season, a time for every purpose under Heaven". There is a time to sow and a time to harvest, a time to celebrate and a time to grieve. There is always a correct time for everything and the Universe knows when that is.

We may think we know the correct time for doing something, but the Universe knows best. This is why we may experience situations where we aren't able to get traction on a project and move forward with it, but at other times we move forward easily and freely.

If we miss an opportunity to do or create something, that opportunity will present itself again, just like the seasons.

The Law of Rhythm encourages us to accept that there is an ideal time for all things.

Affirmation

There is a time for everything I wish to achieve and manifest.

Take some time to contemplate the Law of Rhythm and ask yourself how best you can embody this Universal Law.

19. The Law of Belief

This law deems that whatever you believe you create. Most of us see life the other way around - that our experiences create our beliefs.

For example, if you believe you are not good enough, you will create experiences where you feel not good enough. That experience then reinforces the belief, which keeps creating the same experiences.

A belief may be consciously held or unconsciously held. When we know what the belief is, we have the power to change that belief and therefore change our reality.

The Law of Belief encourages us to become aware of what we believe so that we can change the belief and change the reality we are creating.

Affirmation

What I believe I create.

Take some time to reflect upon this law and your life experiences to date. Ask yourself "what do I have to believe to create this reality?" Choose a different belief!

20. The Law of Gratitude

The Law of Gratitude deems that whatever we feel grateful for, and appreciative of, will expand. When we are in genuine gratitude, we are focusing on what we already have and feeling good about it. From this place we are able to manifest more.

By default, however, we are programmed to constantly notice what is lacking in our lives, and what we haven't got. From this place of lack we cannot manifest anything more. Trying to manifest from a vibration of lack is like trying to grow crops in barren soil. It won't happen!

By practising gratitude on a daily basis, we can shift our mindset from lack to abundance.

The Law of Gratitude encourages us to look at and appreciate all that we already have so as to manifest more.

Affirmation

When I am grateful for all that I have now, I draw to me further abundance.

Contemplate the Law of Gratitude, and ask yourself how can I embrace this law to improve my life?

21. The Law of Healing

We all have the power to heal ourselves, but this ancient knowledge has been lost. When we are connected to Higher Intelligence, we can request healing. Healing is sometimes sent directly through a healing experience or it may be sent through another person. We may be guided on a healing journey of exploration until we are healed.

If a condition or disease is terminal, it is important to note that healing sometimes means finding peace before passing over. The ego likes to think that it has control over how and when we depart. In truth, the soul chooses our exit date.

You can surrender any condition, disease or emotion to the Supreme Intelligence and ask for healing.

The Law of Healing encourages us to have faith in ourselves and our ability to heal.

Affirmation

The Universe has the power to heal me when I request healing.

Reflect on the Law of Healing, and enquire as to how best to utilise this law.

22. The Law of Dharma

The Law of Dharma tells us that we have all incarnated with a purpose, and when we align to that purpose, we shall also receive divinely right abundance.

Your dharma (or purpose) will involve doing something that you love to do and that you are good at. When you do it, you will lose all sense of time and space because you feel at one with life. Your dharma may involve one or more things, and it will reveal itself when you start to become more true to yourself, and follow your heart.

We are all here for different purposes, and so it is pointless to compare yourself and what you do to anyone else and what they do. We are all unique and our dharmas are unique.

The Law of Dharma encourages us to be true to ourselves and our passions.

Affirmation

I am here to find and actuate my purpose.

Take some time to contemplate the Law of Dharma and ask yourself how best you can embrace this law.

23. The Law of Detachment

The Law of Detachment deems that when we detach from an outcome, we allow the Universe to orchestrate in its own way and its own time. This law requires us to detach from an outcome entirely, and be willing to completely let it go, knowing that if it is in our highest good it will come about and if it is not, it won't.

The ego finds it hard to let go, believing that it must cling to an outcome for anything to happen. Detachment requires faith and trust in a loving Universe that only wants what is best for us.

The Law of Detachment encourages us to have absolute faith and trust in Universal Intelligence - that our desired outcome will manifest in divine and perfect timing if it is in our highest good only.

Affirmation

Even though I have desires, I detach from all outcomes.

Reflect upon the Law of Detachment, and enquire as to how best to embrace this law in your life.

24. The Law of Protection

The Supreme Intelligence has the power to protect us and all that we love. When we call upon the Universal Law of Protection and ask that we, our loved ones, our homes and all that we care about be protected, the Universe is onto it.

Knowing this, we can relax and feel peaceful, and we can let go of our need to control everything around us so as to feel safe. The need to control our circumstances comes from our fearful ego that doesn't want to give up control. This is where anxiety comes from.

In handing over all that we love to the Universe for protection, we can rest easy and trust in the process of life.

The Law of Protection encourages us to feel peaceful and trust that the Universe shall protect all that we love if we ask for it.

Affirmation

The Universe has the power to protect all that I love when I ask for protection.

Contemplate the Law of Protection and how you can utilise this powerful law.

25. The Law of Integrity

When you align to the Universal Laws, you align to love, peace and good intentions. Integrity means being integrated with these values through your thoughts, words and actions. Integrity requires that we stay congruent to our truth.

If we break with spiritual law by choosing thoughts, words or actions that are not congruent to what we know is right, good and true, we will be out of our integrity and we will feel the consequences (Law of Karma) as they will have a ripple effect on everything and everyone around us.

Learning to stand in your own integrity will assist you in your healing, growth and evolution.

The Law of Integrity encourages us to stay true to our highest values..

Affirmation

I think, say and do what I know is right and good and true.

Take some time to reflect on the Law of Integrity and how you can bring this law into your life.

Conclusion

It has given me great pleasure to share these laws with you. You may wish to come back to this book from time to time to remind yourself of these Laws of the Universe.

We live in a loving Universe which only wants what is best for us. When we are out of alignment with the Universal Laws, we will create our own consequences. The consequences are our natural lesson; they are not the Universe punishing us.

The more we can honour these laws, the more we shall flourish in every way.

We are all holding ancestral conditioning and old wounding that have created fear and prevented us from knowing these ancient truths, so be kind to yourself as you integrate the Universal Laws and learn new ways of being.

Love and Light,

Nicole x

About the Author

Nicole is an author, spiritual teacher and healer who is based in Sydney, Australia.

Nicole works with people all over the world, facilitating personal transformation.

She has written five books, A Shift to Bliss, 5 Steps to Finding Love, Soul Magic, Soulful & Successful Business and The 25 Universal Laws.

Nicole offers free meditations on the app Insight Timer and her online courses are available from her website.